Lucid Dreaming

LEARN HOW TO CONTROL YOUR DREAMS IN

10 EASY STEPS

CW01497673

By Mia Rose

© **Copyright 2015 by Mia Rose - All rights reserved.**

This document is geared towards providing exact and reliable information in regards to the topic and issue covered. The publication is sold with the idea that the publisher is not required to render accounting, officially permitted, or otherwise, qualified services. If advice is necessary, legal or professional, a practiced individual in the profession should be ordered.

- From a Declaration of Principles which was accepted and approved equally by a Committee of the American Bar Association and a Committee of Publishers and Associations.

In no way is it legal to reproduce, duplicate, or transmit any part of this document in either electronic means or in printed format. Recording of this publication is strictly prohibited and any storage of this document is not allowed unless with written permission from the publisher. All rights reserved.

The information provided herein is stated to be truthful and consistent, in that any liability, in terms of inattention or otherwise, by any usage or abuse of any policies, processes, or directions contained within is the solitary and utter responsibility of the recipient reader. Under no circumstances will any legal responsibility or blame be held against the publisher for any reparation, damages, or monetary loss due to the information herein, either directly or indirectly.

Respective authors own all copyrights not held by the publisher.

The information herein is offered for informational purposes solely, and is universal as so. The presentation of the information is without contract or any type of guarantee assurance.

The trademarks that are used are without any consent, and the publication of the trademark is without permission or backing by the trademark owner. All trademarks and brands within this book are for clarifying purposes only and are the owned by the owners themselves, not affiliated with this document.

Table Of Contents

Table Of Contents..

Introduction..

Chapter 1...

Chapter 2...

Chapter 3...

Chapter 4...

Conclusion...

Preview Of Chakras For Beginners

Check Out My Other Books

About the Author

Introduction

I want to thank you and congratulate you for downloading the book, *"Lucid Dreaming for Beginners"*.

This book contains proven steps and strategies on how to understand the techniques and background behind Lucid Dreaming.

The human brain and mind are the final frontiers when it comes to understanding what we really are as humans. Though science has made great leaps in recent years in understanding how the body and mind work, not every aspect of how the two sides of our consciousness work together is understood. Lucid Dreaming has, however, been documented throughout history and it is a technique that can help you to, literally, double your brain power. Using Lucid Dreaming techniques you can access both sides of your consciousness and harness them both in an effective method to achieve greater understanding of yourself, enhance your problem solving skills, achieve greater creativity and much more. This book looks at what exactly Lucid Dreaming is, the way in which it works and the current thinking on why it works. In addition, there are simple techniques included in the book which will enable anybody to take control of "the other side" of their mind - and put it to good use!

Thanks again for downloading this book, I hope you enjoy it!

Chapter 1

Lucid Dreaming; The Mystery of Being Human

The average human brain weighs in at about three pounds, making it one of the largest organs of the body – roughly joint second with the liver, after our skin. While the rest of our organs – indeed much of how we function – has been poked, prodded, scanned and documented over the last century, our brains remain the final frontier when it comes to understanding what really makes us "us".

MRI scanning has gone a long way to explaining many of the functions of our brain, but scan as hard as you like and it's far more difficult to understand the tantalizingly elusive "mind". Our minds are one of the last great mysteries about us as humans and it's our minds that makes us just that; human. Today, we have at least a better understanding that we have a conscious and subconscious mind. One located in the right hemisphere of our brain and the other in the left. However, by its very nature the subconscious mind is elusive. It operates on a level that is not only hard to scan but is seemingly impossible to access through scans of any kind. The subconscious plays a huge role in creativity, in problem solving and in memory storage. It appears, in some senses, to be our "archive"; the place where our memories and experiences are stored, even if they are not accessible to us in a conscious way. It's also a place where we seem to "process" events in our day-to-day lives and assimilate them into the difficult to define concept that makes us who we are. However, much of this work is done at night – when we're fast asleep, dreaming peacefully and, more or less, completely oblivious to the process!

This part of our brain is normally unaccessible to us in a real sense but in dreams we are effectively "switching" the role of the two sides of our brains. In modern psychology, it's recognized that both elements of consciousness make up our personality but that we only usually have access to one of those sides. During the day, while we are awake, our conscious mind is in charge and at night, our unconscious mind takes over. We experience reality in a completely different way as our dreams create whole new worlds and turn everyday objects into the weird, the wonderful and the sometimes terrifying. However, there are examples throughout history (starting way back with Aristotle) of individuals who appear to retain conscious activity during the nightly dream state. This activity has only been more fully explored in the last forty to fifty years and the term "Lucid Dreaming" has been coined to describe it.

What is Lucid Dreaming?

The term was originally used by the Dutch psychiatrist, Frederik van Eeden, who defined it as meaning "mental clarity". A Lucid Dream is considered to be a dream in which the individual becomes aware that he or she is dreaming and, at this point, is then able to manipulate the events in the dream. During the Lucid Dream, part of the brain reactivates that is responsible for self-awareness – the dorsolateral prefrontal cortex, if you're wondering! Becoming aware that you are dreaming puts you in control of the dream but it also allows you to access that hidden side of your consciousness in a way that is not normally possible. In effect, Lucid Dreaming means that both parts of our brain are active at the same time.

Most people will, at some point in their lives, experience a Lucid Dream. Some experience them frequently, while others only occasionally. Many people also remember their dreams vividly but do not become conscious during the dream. Others, rarely remember their dreams at all. Learning to dream lucidly is, however, possible. In this book we'll take a look at the different techniques and steps you can learn to access your dreams and become conscious during them. We'll also take a look at the benefits of Lucid Dreaming and you may be surprised to learn that apart from being fun, the technique is believed to have some real, practical benefits.

Lucid Dreaming Basics

Before we move on to the benefits and the techniques, it's important to understand clearly what Lucid Dream is and what it isn't as there are many misconceptions.

- Lucid Dreaming is not about being half-awake; this is a very common experience where you wake out of a dream and, in that moment, the dream partly continues as you become aware of the world around you. During a Lucid Dream you are in the REM (rapid eye movement) stage of sleep, completely unconscious of the world around you – or rather the "real" world as we understand it.

- Lucid Dreaming is also sometimes confused with what is known as either an "out of body experience" or Astral Projection. These experiences generally relate to events that happen outside of our own mind and relate to the ability to be present in the real world with what is known as our Astral Body. Lucid Dreaming takes place very much in the individual's own mind.

- Lucid Dreams can be extremely vivid but should not be confused with vivid dreams! In a Lucid Dream, you'll be consciously aware that you are dreaming, while a vivid dream will seem like reality, until you wake and your conscious mind kicks in and you understand that "it was all a dream".

When you learn the art of Lucid Dreaming you become able to access your full range of consciousness – both sides of it. In this state you can explore your own psychology and "meet" parts of you that are not normally accessible to you. These parts often manifest as people and with them you can have deep and very valuable conversations which help to teach you more about yourself.

Chapter 2

Eureka! The Benefits of Lucid Dreaming

Whether Archimedes, attributed with discovering the art of solving problems without actually thinking about them, fell asleep in that elucidating bath, is a fact lost to history. However, simply lying back, relaxing, meditating or even taking a walk and forgetting "the problem" in hand has been an age old technique used to solve problems. Writers, artists, scientists and engineers will often testify that the inspiration that they needed has appeared when they simply stopped looking for it.   Many people, especially those in creative industries, will admit to keeping a notebook by their beds – to jot down any particularly useful dreams.   Most writers will admit to carrying a notebook at all times, as inspiration and ideas can strike at any time, usually not a very convenient one!

Creative Problem Solving and Lucid Dreaming

For most people, at least once in their lives, the experience of waking up with a solution to a problem that had been bothering them is a familiar one. This is, in part, what our unconscious mind seems to be for. If you're facing a problem in life (big or small) the more you focus on it while you are awake the bigger it becomes. The solution also becomes more, and more, elusive. However, fall asleep thinking about it and it's quite possible, that during the night you'll find the solution comes to you. You may not even remember dreaming about the issue (though you probably did) but when you awake your brain has worked through the issues, in a calmer, more rational way, and found the solution.

It's believed that Lucid Dreaming can allow you to access this problem solving side of your mind more directly and more actively. It's also believed that during our unconscious hours we are far better at finding creative solutions to all manner of issues. Studies of the phenomenon are, as yet, few and far between, however, some have already demonstrated (Burke & Shaw[1]) that Lucid Dreamers demonstrate around 25% improvement in problem solving.

While the ability to solve problems while we sleep is possible for anybody (it is, after all, what we do as humans) – accessing the creative, intuitive and imaginative side of our minds and actively being conscious of its operation while we sleep offers us the chance to successfully manipulate our unconscious mind and set it whatever task we choose. Not only improving our general problem solving abilities, this benefit of Lucid Dreaming can help to deal with specific issues rapidly and help us to be simply more efficient in our lives in general.

Stress Relief

Dreams are a time when we process all the things that are happening our life and they are time when we are most naturally relaxed. In terms of relieving stress the jury is still out, but it's likely that Lucid Dreaming may be an effective technique to deal with daily stresses and strains. It also has been suggested that learning the techniques of Lucid Dreaming can also help you to deal with much bigger stress related issues and conditions. On a simple level, if you can control your dream, you can combat stress by dreaming up a holiday for yourself. There are none of the normal bounds to deal with when choosing location; Hawaii, Havana or another planet are all accessible destinations when you master Lucid Dreaming. There's no baggage delays involved and travel is instantaneous! At stressful periods of your life you can book a trip to anywhere that you feel will reduce the stress and you'll be there in a matter of minutes!

On a more serious level, the use of Lucid Dreaming as a technique for combating conditions such as Post-Traumatic-Stress-Disorder (PTSD) has recently been explored. A number of studies have been conducted in recent years and most have concluded that Lucid Dreaming techniques are an effective method for combating nightmares. Although several studies (Spoormaker and van den Bout[2]) have now demonstrated this, it is not yet clear as to how the technique fully works. It does, however, seem that the ability to combat stress in our dreams is a very beneficial side-effect of Lucid Dreaming.

Nightmare Control

Linked to the above, controlling our dreams naturally means that we can "stop" nightmares in their tracks. Nightmares affect us all, at times, and are often the result of our fears (real or imagined) manifesting themselves. Our brains are trying to tell us "what's the worst that could happen" or to play out those fears in the safe environment of sleep. However, for long-term sufferers of nightmares, the experience is far from restful. Being able to control your dreams through conscious participation in them can provide a much needed relief from those nighttime horror movies. This doesn't mean you are avoiding, or blocking, the problem and saving it up for later. Once in control you can deal with the underlying issue that is causing the nightmare in a more beneficial, safe and creative way.

Physical Skills

Learning, or practicing, new physical skills can be exhausting; however, when we're asleep we are fully relaxed. In one study published by Danial Erlacher and Michael Schredl[3] it appeared that Lucid Dreamers who were able to practice a simple task while dreaming could improve their real skills in the waking world. In this study the task consisted of throwing coins into a cup – the participants had to complete this task before going to bed. Lucid Dreamers were asked to continue the practice during their sleep and they were then tested for accuracy once awake and the Lucid Dreamer group showed a marked

2   Psychother Psychosom. 2006;75(6):389-94. Lucid Dreaming treatment for nightmares: a pilot study. Spoormaker VI[1], van den Bout J.

3   TSP Volume 24, Issue 2, June; 157 – 167 Applied Research Practicing a Motor Task in a Lucid Dream Enhances Subsequent Performance: A Pilot Study

improvement in the skill on the previous day. Tossing coins into a cup is a fairly small task. However, many Lucid Dream proponents argue that you can practice any task, sport or activity in your sleep, once you have learned to control your dreams. In reality, this makes sense on several levels; neural pathways form as we practice any skill and, as far as psychologists can tell, our brains don't determine between "real" or "unreal"activity. While some people may believe that this could prove exhausting, Lucid Dreamers report that however active and lucid their dreams are they feel more fully refreshed than ever before when they have mastered the technique.

Fear and Phobias

Most fears and phobias that we experience in life are not as real as they might seem. Fear is a natural human response and it's one that is very useful. However, it can become out of control and when it does so, fear turns to phobia. Lucid Dreaming can be used to battle our phobias and to face them. If you're afraid of heights it's possible to dream of jumping from an impossibly high cliff or from an airplane. Sound scary? In real life it would be but in the dream world, in which you are in control, it becomes a safe, controlled act. You can float, fly or glide down to the ground at your own speed. Lucid Dreamers report that by facing, taking control and acting out their fears they find that their own phobias in real life begin to be less powerful. Again, this is likely to be the result of our brain establishing new neural pathways, experiencing what had formally been fear-inducing in a pleasant way and thereby altering our waking response.

Talking with the Dead

Losing a loved one can be one of the most painful experiences that any of us go through in life. Lucid Dreaming is one technique that can be used to help ease the grief over time. For those who support the technique it's commonly argued that meeting with lost loved ones in our dreams allows us heal on an emotional and psychological level. Even if you simply accept that it's your own psyche that is "creating" the presence, this can give you time and space to actively say the things you need to say and to gradually let go of the individual in question. Lucid Dreaming as a technique for dealing with grief is particularly beneficial where the loss has been sudden or unexpected and it can give us an opportunity to deal with the grief in a productive, creative and positive way in order to find a sense of closure. Again, this is in part to the way in which our brains experience dreams; they make less differentiation between "real" or "not real", perceiving both types of consciousness as different parts of the same reality of experience. When conscious you may realize your encounter with a loved one was a dream, but in your deeper mind the experience will stick and register as real. It may be interesting to note that many people actually seem to experience this type of Lucid Dream in what may be best described as a "waking dream". After a sudden loss it is normal to "see" and talk with the lost loved one. Psychologists have no qualms about accepting this experience as real, simply seeing it as a coping mechanism to aid us in our grieving process. Actively utilizing this technique through Lucid Dreaming can be very beneficial indeed.

Creative Expressions

Humans are creative by nature – we'd not have got to where we are without our creative sides. However, not all of us are as in touch with this aspect of our personality as others. In fact, it's believed that many of our creative abilities are controlled within the subconscious – that this is the creative side of the brain. When we use Lucid Dreaming techniques we are in direct contact with this side of our brain and we can begin to access it at will. The free flow of ideas that comes from this part of consciousness can be inspiring and also extremely enlightening. Lucid Dreamers often experience a change in focus in their lives and find that they have hidden, creative talents that they'd never imagined. Any area of life which requires creativity (and most do) can be enhanced through Lucid Dreaming Techniques.

Chapter 3

Lucid Dreaming; The Practicalities

There are a number of scientific facts that it's worth understanding about sleep and dreaming before learning the techniques of Lucid Dreaming. In this chapter we'll take you through the basics of sleep, dreams and the types of Lucid Dream that you can expect to experience as you practice the steps we have described later in this book.

False Awakening

This is often seen as a type of Lucid Dream but is not, in fact, real Lucid Dreaming. In this type of dream the individual "awakes" finding themselves in a room that is similar, or the same, as the one in which they would expect to be (the room in which they went to bed). Often the individual begins their normal, daily, morning routine but this is interrupted when they awake again; this can be another false awakening or the real thing. Only at this point does the consciousness kick in and the individual will realize that they have been dreaming.

Sleep Paralysis

Again, this condition is sometimes mistaken for Lucid Dreaming but usually occurs in a half-awake state, somewhere between full and half consciousness. During sleep our body becomes paralyzed. This is a self-protection technique to stop us from physically acting out the events of our dream. This occurs during normal sleep, normal dreaming and during Lucid Dreaming (so don't worry!). During this state the individual may awaken feeling that they cannot move and also experience "hypnagogic" hallucinations. These are uncontrolled visions, sounds or sensations that originate in our subconscious; sounds are particularly common and one frequently reported auditory (sound) hallucination that is reported is hearing someone calling your name. Many of those who practice Lucid Dreaming find that incidences of sleep paralysis – the experience of awaking while still in this state become more frequent or more pronounced. This can be disturbing at first – both the paralysis and the sounds/images – but is a perfectly normal function of the body and mind and should not be a cause for worry or fear.

Prompting Lucid Dreams

There are three generally accepted ways in which we can enter a Lucid Dream state. These are;

- Dream Initiation of Lucid Dreams (DILD)

- Mnemonic Initiation of Lucid Dreams (MILD)

- Waking Initiation of Lucid Dreams (WILD)

DILD

This is the most natural way in which Lucid Dreams occur and the one through which the majority of individuals will first experience the phenomenon. The dreamer falls asleep naturally and begins to dream. During the dream the conscious part of the brain (or parts of it) reactive naturally and the dreamer becomes aware that they are dreaming. These dreams are often characterized by their mundane nature. The events of the dream will be either every day or, at least, not unusual. Some aspect of the dream may seem odd, or the experience may be unfamiliar. As the dreamer realizes that they are dreaming they begin to experience some sense of control and can begin to shape the events in the dream. This type of Lucid Dream is the one that most will experience, however, there are no demonstrable techniques for achieving it. While it will almost certainly happen at some stage in your life this most natural form of Lucid Dreaming is the one that it is hardest to achieve.

MILD

This technique was pioneered by Stephen LaBerge, a leading expert in the field of Lucid Dreaming. The technique operates by training the mind to identify that you are dreaming. This is, surprisingly, relatively easy! The technique involves simply creating a habit while you are awake and continuing this while you are dreaming. The activity itself should then be recognized as an indication that you are now dreaming. This may sound complicated but it's relatively simple. Habits or tasks that are suggested include counting your fingers while you are awake – ideally once you are in bed. Look at each finger and try to get a good mental image of them in your mind. Keep counting and looking for a few minutes and then try to relax and fall asleep. Once asleep the brain begins its task of ordering and analyzing the day's events. It may, or may not, deal with the last thing first! However, using this technique will normally lead to some success. The visual aspect of your perception is important here; in the dream the fingers may appear to be rather more numerous than they should be or some may be missing. This is your cue to realize that you are dreaming. When the realization comes this is the point that parts of your conscious mind are re-activated and the point at which you can begin to control the dream. The "MILD" technique is particularly good for beginners and can be effective within days or weeks of learning.

WILD

More complex and harder to master than MILD, this technique may require some practice. In DILD and MILD techniques of initiating Lucid Dreaming the individual falls asleep normally, dreams and then part of their consciousness switches back on. In this technique the aim is keep your consciousness "switched on" as you fall asleep and enter directly into a dream state. Effective methods of achieving this are meditation and relaxation techniques with the aim being to simply fall asleep with your mind still partly focused and conscious. There are certain points in the sleep cycle where this technique can be particularly effective. If REM is interrupted it will restart immediately when you fall asleep. By waking yourself earlier than normal and then falling back asleep, or simply getting up and taking a nap later in the day, you'll prompt a state where dreaming will begin almost instantaneously. Combining this with a relaxation technique to help your body achieve sleep quickly can be an effective to simply enter a Lucid Dream directly.

Note: this technique is the most likely in which you'll experience sleep paralysis as you fall asleep. You may experience loss of movement, a sensation of falling and/or strange visions and sounds. This is perfectly normal (it happens every time we fall asleep) but under normal circumstances we don't experience it consciously. Be prepared for a strange experience or two if you practice this method!

Chapter 4

Top Ten Lucid Dreaming Techniques

In this final section we'll take a look at simple techniques and exercises you can use to begin your journey with Lucid Dreaming. The techniques are based on the three main ways to enter a Lucid Dreaming state, as described in the previous chapter. For those new to Lucid Dreaming, the easiest techniques include those that fall under the MILD category and you can normally use these to induce Lucid Dreams very quickly (if you've experienced many natural or DIDL events in your life you'll find that inducing them can be accomplished in a matter of days, possibly only one). It's also possible to combine some of these different techniques in order to create the right environment for Lucid Dreaming to occur, simply read through and try out one (or several) of the techniques which most appeal to you.

Technique 1: Focus on Lucid Dreaming

Your brain is surprisingly simple to manipulate! If you've ever tried to find the solution to a problem (either on purpose or by accident) by thinking about it before you go to sleep then you'll realize just how easy. For this technique simply think about the subject of Lucid Dreaming; talk about it, read about it (use this book and online resources from those who have experienced Lucid Dreams), think about it all day! This creates a mental focus on the subject and is likely to be a strong factor in prompting the real thing. This technique can be used on its own but it's ideal for using on a day-to-day basis and should simply become part of your normal routine. Particularly focus on it before going to sleep.

Technique 2: That "Am I Dreaming" Moment

This is the question you need to ask when you are asleep in order to become lucid in your dreams. Training yourself to ask that question is fairly simple, just ask it all the time. The more you do, the more likely it is to filter across into your brain once you are! You should ask the question throughout the day and it's a good idea to have a visual clue to compare between the two states of waking or sleeping. Clues can include a letter or word written on your hand; "A" or "Awake". Keep asking the question and checking for the answer on your hand! The nature of dreams means that you'll most likely continue the checks once asleep but that the "answer" may have changed to "D" or "Dreaming". It may also have disappeared, but in some way there will be a subtle clue. At this point you'll become aware that you are now dreaming and can begin to explore the other side of your conscious world.

Technique 3: "Return to the Dark Ages"

Well not quite, perhaps, but simply inducing natural sleep will help to ensure that the transition from waking to sleeping (and hence dreaming) is rapid. This technique requires some sacrifice (for many of us) and involves turning off all non-natural light sources a good hour before you go to bed. This includes TVs, computers of every kind (including) smart phones and, if possible, most electric lighting. You can simply burn a candle (be sure to be safe) or have a single, low light source in the room. The light emitted by all of our modern gadgetry mimics natural daylight and this stops our bodies from producing natural sleep hormones (disrupting our natural body clock). You can spend this quiet time relaxing, meditating or practicing breathing exercises, all of which will help to induce the correct state to facilitate Lucid Dreaming. When retiring for the night, go straight to bed and simply allow your body to relax and drift off. Don't try to force sleep as this will have the opposite effect; if you've spent an hour allowing your body to prepare for sleep in this natural way, it should come quickly. One side-benefit of this technique is that it's also an excellent way to induce healthy, natural sleep which can have enormous benefits for your physical and mental health as well as making you feel more refreshed the next day!

this technique will initiate a Lucid Dream on the very first attempt, although the dream may be fleeting. With practice your control and the length of the dream should become better established. This technique can be combined with several of the others and can be particularly effective combined with technique number 2.

Technique 8: Dream Reenactment

If you have clear memories of your dreams, or begin to develop these by keeping a dream diary, you can practice Lucid Dreaming while you are awake! Simply remember a recent dream but change the ending of the dream to an alternative ending, or one that you would prefer. Do this in a quiet place where you won't be disturbed and focus on a dream from as recently as possible (the previous night being the best option). As you explore the dream and your new ending keep telling yourself that you are dreaming. This trains your brain while you are conscious into the habit of recognizing dreams and becoming conscious that they are only dreams. Practice as often as you can, before going to bed is a good time as it gets the habit ingrained in your brain at the right time of day! With time, you'll find that you become more aware of your conscious mind during future dreams and will also find that it becomes easier to alter the course of those dreams as you do.

Technique 9: Stay with It

When you first practice Lucid Dreaming you may find that the period of lucidity is short-lived. You recognize you are dreaming and are able to influence the dream consciously but soon lose the sense of control and the understanding that you are dreaming at all. Learning to manipulate, influence and change your dreams takes practice. When you begin to achieve Lucid Dreams simply learn to stay calm and to control your environment within the dream. Talk to yourself (nobody is listening) calmly and focus on objects, people or elements of the dream. If you meet somebody talk to them about the fact that you are dreaming (and dreaming them) and see how they respond. Pick up objects or move things around mentally in the dream. Try to simply change the setting. Always remain calm; if the dream is verging on a nightmare simply focus on a positive outcome and "remind" the dream that you are in charge. When it comes to people that you meet in your dreams there are several types of character – although ultimately they are all "you". As mentioned in the previous chapter you may meet "real" people who you have lost in real life. This is your subconscious helping you to "finish" conversations or to tell them things that you may not have done in life. Simply start those conversations or say the words that you need to. Other characters are you in a deeper sense, they are manifestations of your psyche and these can be useful people to meet. They can help you understand more about yourself and find solutions to issues or problems in life. Ask them who they are, explain that you know that you are dreaming and that they are part of you, ask which part, what they have to tell you and why. This kind of discussion can be a powerful self-growth tool and also a great way to keep control of the dream and remain conscious.

Technique 10: Technological Enhancement

During Lucid Dreaming studies one technique that has been discovered to alert dreamers that they are, in fact, dreaming, is the use of light or auditory stimulation. Devices are available which detect REM stages of sleep and produce a small visual or auditory effect which is designed to "filter" into the dream and to then be recognized by the dreamer as a clue to the fact that they are dreaming. The signals are not strong enough to arouse the individual from sleep but to prompt a response within the dream. This response is very similar to being aware of a radio, alarm or smart-phone alarm while you continue to sleep. If you've ever experienced the noises, speech or music playing in the real world intruding into, and being incorporated into, your dreams then you've already experienced this effect. You can purchase these devices online but you can also simply try using a radio, on a low setting, to prompt the same effect of weaving the "real" into the unreal world.

And, Finally

Lucid Dreaming is a well-documented fact and one that has been practiced for different purposes for many centuries (probably longer). It's possible for anyone to experience Lucid Dreams and most of us do so naturally at some point in our lives. However, learning to consistently practice Lucid Dreaming can take time and patience. Use the tips above to train your brain to recognize the difference between waking reality and dreaming reality. In some cases, this lesson will be rapid and you'll soon have great control of your dreams. In others it can take more time but will come, given practice and perseverance.

Dreams can be wonderful, fun and exciting and when you can learn to control them this is more likely than ever to be the case. However, sometimes dreams can become nightmares, literally, in this case. Do not, at any point, be afraid. Whenever you experience more negative dreams and nightmares simply practice taking control. Everything that is happening in your dream is in your mind and you have absolute control of the experience. You can even learn, with time to wake yourself up if necessary. While in a Lucid Dream simply tell yourself "I need to wake up now" and you will do so. You may either wake up in reality or experience a false awakening but, either way, you should recognize that the dream (or the previous one) was nothing more than that and has no power to harm you.

Conclusion

Thank you again for downloading this book!

I hope this book was able to help you to understand what Lucid Dreaming is and how it can benefit your life.

The next step is to put into practice some, or all, of the techniques described in the book and to start to access the other side of your mind. I wish you every success with Lucid Dreaming and hope that it will aid you in growing your mind, your creativity and your mental abilities!

Finally, if you enjoyed this book, please take the time to share your thoughts and post a review on Amazon. It'd be greatly appreciated!

Thank you and good luck!

Preview of Chakras For Beginners

The ancient study of Chakras has made its way into the western world as of late. Frequently the first exposure can come through the study of yoga, meditation or hindu practices.

The body and every living being is filled with a universal energy that connects and surrounds us.This energy can has been described as being made up of 7 layers (Auras) and the 7 chakras (energy points or knots in the body)

The book is designed for those new to the concept but will also be useful for those with some experience of Chakra and energy healing. In the next chapter we take a more detailed look at what the Chakras are, and an overview of each one of the seven main Chakras. The remaining part of the book looks at each individual Chakra and how to examine the Chakra for imbalances. The final chapter provides a simple list-style section of tools that traditional (and modern) Chakra experts believe are useful in achieving balance within your Chakra energy system.

When our Chakras are in balance they allow energy to freely flow through our bodies and keep us revitalized, healthy and connected to the world around us. However, imbalances within the Chakra system can cause the energy to become blocked, leading to ill health both physical and emotional.

Here Is a Preview of What you'll learn...

- History Of Chakras
- What Chakras Are
- In-depth Description Of Each Chakra
- Causes Of Chakra Imbalances
- Chakra Test
- How To Balance Each Chakra

Check Out My Other Books

Below you'll find some of my other popular books that are popular on Amazon and Kindle as well. Simply click on the links below to check them out. Alternatively, you can visit my author page on Amazon to see other works done by me.

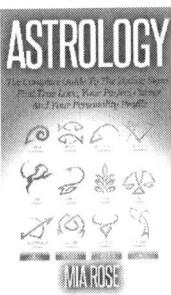

http://www.amazon.com/Astrology-Complete-Perfect-Personality-Horoscope-ebook/dp/B00N6HWV6K

http://www.amazon.com/Chakras-Beginners-Understanding-Sprituality-Meditation-ebook/dp/B00LNC6YGS

http://www.amazon.com/Crystals-Ultimate-Crystal-Healing-Spirituality-ebook/dp/B00SWMDP46

http://www.amazon.com/Numerology-Ultimate-Uncovering-Creating-Horoscope-ebook/dp/B00O6HWE8O

About the Author

I want to thank you for giving me the opportunity to spend some time with you!

For the last 10 years of my life I have studied, practiced and shared my love of spirituality and internal development. I kept diaries for years documenting the incredible changes that graced my life. This passion for writing has blossomed into a new chapter in my life where publishing books has become a full time career.

I feel extremely blessed and fortunate to have the opportunity to share my message with you! Each of my books are written to inspire others to explore the many aspects of their internal world. My goal is to touch the lives of others in a positive way and hopefully be the catalyst of positive change in this world :)

I am forever grateful for your support and I know you will get immense value through my books. I am really looking forward to serve you and give you great insight into my passions!

Your Friend

Mia   Rose

22772859R00019

Printed in Great Britain
by Amazon